Hun

by Iain Gray

Lang**Syne**

PUBLISHING

WRITING *to* REMEMBER

Lang**Syne**

PUBLISHING

WRITING *to* REMEMBER

79 Main Street, Newtongrange,
Midlothian EH22 4NA
Tel: 0131 344 0414   Fax: 0845 075 6085
E-mail: info@lang-syne.co.uk
www.langsyneshop.co.uk

Design by Dorothy Meikle
Printed by Printwell Ltd
© Lang Syne Publishers Ltd 2017

ISBN 978-1-85217-663-1

Humphreys

MOTTO:
The true man loves his country.

CREST:
An otter wounded in the shoulder.

NAME variations include:
Homfray
Humfrey
Humfreys
Humfrie
Humfries
Humphries
Humpherson
Humphrey
Humphreyson
Humphry

Chapter one:

Origins of
Welsh surnames

by Iain Gray

***If you don't know where you came from, you won't
know where you're going*** **is a frequently quoted
observation and one that has a particular resonance
today when there has been a marked upsurge in
interest in genealogy, with increasing numbers of
people curious to trace their family roots.**

Main sources for genealogical research include
census returns and official records of births, marriages
and deaths – and the key to unlocking the detail they
contain is obviously a family surname, one that has been
'inherited' and passed from generation to generation.

No matter our station in life, we all have a
surname – but it was not until about the middle of the
fourteenth century that the practice of being identified
by a particular, or 'fixed', surname became commonly
established throughout the British Isles.

Previous to this, it was normal for a person to
be identified through the use of only a forename.

Wales, however, known in the Welsh language as *Cymru*, is uniquely different – with the use of what are known as patronymic names continuing well into the fifteenth century and, in remote rural areas, up until the early nineteenth century.

Patronymic names are ones where a son takes his father's forename, or Christian name, as his surname.

Examples of patronymic names throughout the British Isles include 'Johnson', indicating 'son of John', while specifically in Scotland 'son of' was denoted by the prefix Mc or Mac – with 'MacDonald', for example, meaning 'son of Donald.'

Early Welsh law, known as *Cyfraith Hywel*, *The Law of Hywel*, introduced by Hywel the Good, who ruled from Prestatyn to Pembroke between 915 AD and 950 AD, stipulated that a person's name should indicate their ancestry – the name in effect being a type of 'family tree.'

This required the prefixes *ap* or *ab* – derived from *mab*, meaning 'son of' being placed before the person's baptismal name.

In the case of females, the suffixes *verch* or *ferch*, sometimes shortened to *vch* or *vz* would be attached to their Christian name to indicate 'daughter of.'

In some cases, rather than being known for

example as *Llewellyn ap Thomas* – *Llewellyn son of Thomas* – Llewellyn's name would incorporate an 'ancestral tree' going back much earlier than his father.

One source gives the example of *Llewellyn ap Thomas ap Dafydd ap Evan ap Owen ap John* – meaning *Llewellyn son of Thomas son of Dafydd son of Evan son of Owen son of John*.

This leads to great confusion, to say the least, when trying to trace a person's ancestry back to a particular family – with many people having the forenames, for example, of Llewellyn, Thomas, Owen or John.

The first Act of Union between Wales and England that took place in 1536 during the reign of Henry VIII required that all Welsh names be registered in an Anglicised form – with *Hywel*, for example, becoming Howell, or Powell, and *Gruffydd* becoming Griffiths.

An early historical example of this concerns William ap John Thomas, standard bearer to Henry VIII, who became William Jones.

In many cases – as in Davies and Williams – an s was simply added to the original patronymic name, while in other cases the prefix *ap* or *ab* was contracted to *p* or *b* to prefix the name – as in *ab Evan* to form Bevan and *ap Richard* to form Pritchard.

Other original Welsh surnames – such as Morgan, originally *Morcant* – derive from ancient Celtic sources, while others stem from a person's physical characteristics – as in *Gwyn* or *Wynne* a nickname for someone with fair hair, *Gough* or *Gooch* denoting someone with red hair or a ruddy complexion, *Gethin* indicating swarthy or ugly and *Lloyd* someone with brown or grey hair.

With many popular surnames found today in Wales being based on popular Christian names such as John, this means that what is known as the 'stock' or 'pool' of names is comparatively small compared to that of common surnames found in England, Scotland and Ireland.

This explains why, in a typical Welsh village or town with many bearers of a particular name not necessarily being related, they were differentiated by being known, for example, as 'Jones the butcher', 'Jones the teacher' and 'Jones the grocer.'

Another common practice, dating from about the nineteenth century, was to differentiate among families of the same name by prefixing it with the mother's surname or hyphenating the name.

The history of the origins and development of Welsh surnames is inextricably bound up with the nation's frequently turbulent history and its rich culture.

Speaking a Celtic language known as Brythonic, which would gradually evolve into Welsh, the natives were subjected to Roman invasion in 48 AD, and in the following centuries to invasion by the Anglo-Saxons, Vikings and Normans.

Under England's ruthless and ambitious Edward I, the nation was fortified with castles between 1276 and 1295 to keep the 'rebellious' natives in check – but this did not prevent a series of bloody uprisings against English rule that included, most notably, Owain Glyndŵr's rebellion in 1400.

Politically united with England through the first Act of Union in 1536, becoming part of the Kingdom of Great Britain in 1707 and part of the United Kingdom in 1801, it was in 1999 that *Cynulliad Cenedlaethol Cymru*, the National Assembly for Wales, was officially opened by the Queen.

Welsh language and literature has flourished throughout the nation's long history.

In what is known as the Heroic Age, early Welsh poets include the late sixth century Taliesin and Aneirin, author of *Y Gododdin*.

Discovered in a thirteenth century manuscript but thought to date from anywhere between the seventh and eleventh centuries, it refers to the kingdom of Gododdin that took in south-east Scotland and

Northumberland and was part of what was once the Welsh territory known as *Hen Ogledd*, *The Old North*.

Commemorating Gododdin warriors who were killed in battle against the Angles of Bernicia and Deira at Catraith in about 600 AD, the manuscript – known as *Llyfr Aneirin*, *Book of Aneirin* – is now in the precious care of Cardiff City Library.

Other important early works by Welsh poets include the fourteenth century *Red Book of Hergest*, now held in the Bodleian Library, Oxford, and the *White Book of Rhydderch*, kept in the National Library of Wales, Aberystwyth.

William Morgan's translation of the Bible into Welsh in 1588 is hailed as having played an important role in the advancement of the Welsh language, while in 1885 Dan Isaac Davies founded the first Welsh language society.

It was in 1856 that Evan James and his son James James composed the rousing Welsh national anthem *Hen Wlad Fynhadad – Land of My Fathers*, while in the twentieth century the poet Dylan Thomas gained international fame and acclaim with poems such as *Under Milk Wood*.

The nation's proud cultural heritage is also celebrated through *Eisteddfod Genedlaethol Cymru*, the National Eisteddfod of Wales, the annual festival of music, literature and performance that is held across the nation and which traces its roots back to 1176 when Rhys ap Gruffyd, who ruled the territory of Deheubarth from 1155 to 1197, hosted a magnificent festival of poetry and song at his court in Cardigan.

The 2011 census for Wales unfortunately shows that the number of people able to speak the language has declined from 20.8% of the population of just under 3.1 million in 2001 to 19% – but overall the nation's proud culture, reflected in its surnames, still flourishes.

Many Welsh families proudly boast the heraldic device known as a Coat of Arms, as featured on our front cover.

The central motif of the Coat of Arms would originally have been what was borne on the shield of a warrior to distinguish himself from others on the battlefield.

Not featured on the Coat of Arms, but highlighted on page three, is the family motto and related crest – with the latter frequently different from the central motif.

Echoes of a far distant past can still be found in our surnames and they can be borne with pride in commemoration of our forebears.

Chapter two:

Invasion and conquest

Derived from the Old French given name 'Humfrey', 'Humphreys' in turn derives from the Old German names 'Hunfrid' and 'Humfrid' – with 'hun' meaning 'bear cub' and 'frid', or 'fred', indicating 'peace'.

As a surname, with the final 's' indicating 'son of', Humphreys and its popular spelling variations that include Humphries and Humphrys was popularised in the wake of the Norman Conquest of 1066.

One reason for the popularity of 'Humfrey' as a forename was through reverence by those Normans – who settled at the point of a sword in England and subsequently in Wales – for the ninth century St Humfrey of Therouanne, in France.

It was the Conquest of 1066, meanwhile, that sounded the death knell of not only Anglo-Saxon control of England but ultimately also of Welsh independence.

By this date, England had become a nation with several powerful competitors to the throne.

In what were extremely complex family, political and military machinations, the monarch was Harold II, who had succeeded to the throne following the death of Edward the Confessor.

But his right to the kingship was contested by two powerful competitors – his brother-in-law King Harold Hardrada of Norway, in alliance with Tostig, Harold II's brother, and Duke William II of Normandy.

On October 14, Harold II encountered a mighty invasion force led by Duke William that had landed at Hastings, in East Sussex.

He drew up a strong defensive position, at the top of Senlac Hill, building a shield wall to repel William's cavalry and infantry.

The Normans suffered heavy losses, but through a combination of the deadly skill of their archers and the ferocious determination of their cavalry they eventually won the day.

Anglo-Saxon morale had collapsed on the battlefield as word spread through the ranks that Harold, the last of the Anglo-Saxon kings, had been killed.

William was declared King of England on December 25, and the complete subjugation of his Anglo-Saxon subjects followed, with those Normans who had fought on his behalf rewarded with lands – a pattern that would be repeated in Wales.

Invading across the Welsh Marches, the borderland between England and Wales, the Normans gradually consolidated gains by building castles – while under a succession of Welsh leaders who included

Llywelyn ap Gruffudd, known as Llywelyn the Last, resistance proved strong.

But it was brutally crushed in 1283 under England's ruthless and ambitious Edward I, who ordered the building or repair of at least 17 castles and in 1302 proclaimed his son and heir, the future Edward II, as Prince of Wales, a title known in Welsh as *Tywysog Cymru*.

A heroic Welsh figure arose from 1400 to 1415 in the form of Owain Glyndŵr – the last native Welshman to be recognised by his supporters as *Tywysog Cymru*.

In what is known as The Welsh Revolt he achieved an early series of stunning victories against Henry IV and his successor Henry V – until mysteriously disappearing from the historical record after mounting an ambush in Brecon.

Some sources assert that he was either killed in the ambush or died a short time afterwards from wounds he received – but there is a persistent tradition that he survived and lived thereafter in anonymity, protected by loyal followers.

During the revolt, he had consistently refused offers of a Royal Pardon and – despite offers of hefty rewards for his capture – he was never betrayed.

It is in Denbighshire, in the south-east of Wales and one of its thirteen historic counties, that those who were to assume 'Humphreys' as a surname are particularly identified – with, in the form of 'Humphrey', a William Humphrey recorded there in 1240.

Denbighshire, the oldest inhabited part of Wales and known in Welsh as *Sir Ddinbych* – with 'Sir' denoting 'County' – was created through the Laws of Wales Acts of 1535 and 1542.

This was from areas previously in the Welsh Marches, and today the landscape is still dominated by imposing edifices such as Rhuddlan Castle, Denbigh Castle and Bodelwyddan Castle.

But it was not only in the early Humphreys' Welsh heartland of Denbighshire that bearers of the name stamped their mark on the historical record.

Born in 1571 in the English county of Hampshire, Laurence Humphreys was the English Catholic martyr and saint who had converted from the Protestant faith when he was aged eighteen.

In common with many other religious converts, he was particularly zealous in his devotion to his new-found faith and, in his case, highly critical of the Protestant Queen Elizabeth, daughter of Henry VIII through his ill-fated second wife Anne Boleyn.

Struck with a serious illness in 1591, in a fevered and delirious state Humphreys was heard to call the queen 'a harlot and heretic.'

Arrested and dragged off to imprisonment in Winchester, at his trial later that year he claimed to have no recollection of what he had said – but he damned himself by stating that he did not dispute the evidence against him and was willing to be punished.

Condemned and executed for High Treason, it was nearly 340 years later, in 1929, that he was beatified by Pope Pius XI, while his feast day is July 7.

From religious belief to political belief, and in much later times, Christine Humphreys, more properly known as Baroness Humphreys, is a prominent Welsh Liberal Democrat.

Elected president of the Welsh Liberal Democrats in 2007, she was a Member of the National Assembly for Wales for the North Wales constituency from 1999 to 2001.

A former teacher, she was created a life peer in 2013, taking the title Baroness Humphreys, of Llanrwst in the County of Conway.

In twentieth century American politics, Hubert Humphreys was the Democratic Party politician who served under President Lyndon B. Johnson from 1965 to 1969 as 38th Vice President of the United States.

Born in 1911 in Wallace, South Dakota, the former pharmacist – who represented Minnesota in the United States Senate – died in 1978.

Chapter three:

Crime and punishment

Two bearers of the Humphreys name feature prominently in the dark annals of criminal justice.

They are the grandly named Sir Richard Somers Travers Christmas Humphreys and his son Travers Christmas Humphreys, both of whom sat in judgement on a number of highly controversial British court cases.

Born in 1867 in Bloomsbury, London, the fourth son and sixth child of a solicitor, Richard Humphreys' mother was a sister of the nineteenth century English stage entertainer Richard Corney Grain.

Graduating from Cambridge University when he was aged 22 and called to the Bar, Humphreys' first major foray into the realms of criminal justice came in 1895 when he acted as a junior counsel for the prosecution in the celebrated case of *Wilde v Queensbury*.

The Wilde in question was none other than the flamboyant author and dramatist Oscar Wilde, while 'Queensbury' was John Sholto Douglas, the 9th Marquess of Queensbury who gave his name to the 'Queensbury rules' that govern modern boxing.

It was after Queensbury – with whose son,

Lord Alfred Douglas, Wilde had an intense relationship – left the writer a calling card inscribed 'For Oscar Wilde, posing sodomite', that Wilde sued him for criminal libel.

Queensbury was duly arrested on a charge of criminal libel – one that carried a possible sentence of up to two years imprisonment – and the case came to trial in April of 1895.

The evidence presented by the defence that Wilde was indeed a sodomite was convincing, at least in the eyes of the jury, and Queensbury was acquitted.

Under the Libel Act, this meant Wilde not only became liable for the massive costs of the trial, but also open to arrest on charges of gross indecency and sodomy.

Brought to trial, he was found guilty and sentenced to two years' hard labour.

First confined in Wandsworth Prison and then Pentonville Prison, he was later transferred to Reading Prison, where he penned his famous poem *The Ballad of Reading Gaol*.

In 1910, Humphreys appeared as junior counsel in the prosecution of Hawley Harvey Crippen, better known to posterity as Dr Crippen, the American-born homeopath, ear and eye specialist and pharmacist who was found guilty of the murder of his wife Cora in their home in Holloway, London.

With a warrant out for his arrest and wanted posters of Crippen and his lover Ethel Neave distributed by Scotland Yard, he attempted to evade justice by crossing the Atlantic aboard the transatlantic liner *Montrose*.

But the alert captain of the vessel recognised Crippen and Neave from the wanted posters and duly alerted the authorities via transatlantic wireless telegram – the first time the telegraph had ever been put to such use.

Police boarded the *Montrose* as it entered the St Lawrence River, in Canada, which was then a dominion of the British Empire, and arrested Crippen.

Returned to England for trial and with Humphreys one of the prosecution team, Crippen was found guilty and hanged in Pentonville Prison in November of 1910.

Five years later, Humphreys was one of the prosecution team in the trial of the English serial killer and bigamist George Joseph Smith.

In what was dubbed by the press as "The Brides in the Bath Murders", Smith was convicted at the Old Bailey of the murder of three women for financial gain by drowning them in bathtubs and subsequently hanged.

In the 2003 television drama *The Brides in the*

Bath, Humphreys was portrayed by the actor Ian Connaughton.

Sitting as a judge in the Court of Criminal Appeal, Humphreys was involved in the case of William Brooke Joyce in his appeal against conviction for High Treason.

Nicknamed "Lord Haw-Haw" because of his upper class English accent, the American-born Irish-British fascist had been convicted at the end of the Second World War in 1945 for having acted as a Nazi propaganda broadcaster to the United Kingdom.

The Court of Criminal Appeal and the House of Lords both upheld the conviction and Joyce was hanged in Wandsworth Prison.

In 1949, Humphreys presided over the trial of John George Haigh, the English serial killer who had been accused of murdering six women for financial gain.

Sensationally dubbed "The Acid Bath Murderer" by the press, Haigh had disposed of his victims' bodies by immersing them in concentrated sulphuric acid.

With Haigh found guilty, Humphreys solemnly donned his black cap and sentenced him to be hanged.

The judge died in 1956, while he was the father of the equally noted Travers Christmas Humphreys, who prosecuted a number of cases in the

1940s and 1950s before becoming a judge at the Old Bailey.

Born in 1901, one particularly infamous case over which he presided was that of the Welshman Timothy Evans, wrongly convicted and subsequently hanged in March of 1950 for the murder of his wife and infant child.

It subsequently emerged that the murders had been committed by John Christie, now known to have killed at least six women, including his wife, between 1943 and 1953.

Born in 1899 in Halifax, West Yorkshire, and having married and settled by the outbreak of the Second World War in a flat at 10 Rillington Place, in the Notting Hill area of London, Christie had a string of previous convictions for assault and theft – but police failed to check this before accepting him for Special Constable duties.

It was not until he moved out of 10 Rillington Place in March of 1953 that new tenants discovered the bodies of three of his victims hidden in a kitchen alcove, while others were later discovered buried in a backyard and hidden in a wash-house.

One of the bodies was identified as that of his wife, Ethel, and it was for her murder that he was hanged in July of 1953.

It subsequently emerged that some of his victims were usually strangled by Christie in his flat after he had rendered them unconscious by administering domestic gas while supposedly, in some cases, raping them – many of the unsuspecting women having come to him to obtain an abortion.

In a controversy that persists to this day, Christie had been a key prosecution witness in the trial of Timothy Evans.

Born in Merthyr Tydfil, Glamorgan in 1924, he and his wife Beryl had been tenants of Christie during 1948 and 1949 – and it emerged later that it was he, not Evans, who had murdered Evans' wife and infant child.

Evans was consequently granted a posthumous pardon in October of 1966, while the miscarriage of justice is considered to have significantly contributed a year before his pardon to the abolition of capital punishment for murder in the United Kingdom.

Richard Attenborough later chillingly portrayed Christie in the 1977 film *10 Rillington Place*, based in part on the book of the same name by the late campaigning journalist and author Ludovic Kennedy, while John Hurt portrayed the hapless Timothy Evans.

Equally controversially, Humphreys also presided over the trial of Ruth Ellis, convicted in 1955 of the murder of her lover David Blakely by shooting him outside a public house in Hampstead, London.

Sentenced to death by Humphreys and hanged in Holloway Prison, she was the last woman to be executed in the United Kingdom.

Appointed a Commissioner at the Old Bailey in 1962, Christmas Humphreys provoked a public outcry in 1975 when he passed an astonishingly lean six-month suspended jail sentence on an 18-year-old man who had raped two women at knife-point.

With pressure mounting on him, including a House of Commons motion for the Lord Chancellor to dismiss him, Humphreys resigned six months later.

A convert to Buddhism, having founded the London Buddhist Society in 1924 and a prolific author on the subject, the highly colourful and controversial Christmas Humphreys died in 1983.

Chapter four:

On the world stage

**Bearers of the Humphreys name and its popular
spelling variants of Humphries and Humphrys have
achieved fame and celebrity through a diverse range
of endeavours and pursuits.**

Born in Ontario in 1953, **Alfred Humphreys** is
the Canadian actor of television and film whose first
major screen role was that of Deputy Lester in the 1982
First Blood, starring Sylvester Stallone as Rambo.

Other roles include that of Howard Landers in
the 1981 *My Bloody Valentine*, while other credits include
the 2003 *X2* and the 2010 *Diary of a Wimpy Kid*, while
he has also made guest appearances on television's *The
X-Files* and *The Twilight Zone*.

A British actor of theatre and film, **Cecil
Humphreys** was born in 1883 in Cheltenham,
Gloucestershire.

A noted Broadway actor between the 1920s
and the 1940s, he also appeared in nearly fifty films
between 1916 and 1948 that included the 1939
Wuthering Heights, starring with Laurence Olivier, the
1946 *The Razor's Edge* and, released only a few months
after his death, the 1948 *A Woman's Vengeance*.

He was the grandfather of the Canadian-British actor, playwright and novelist **Chris Humphreys**, born in Toronto, and who settled in Britain with his family when he was aged seven.

Best known for his role from 1989 to 1990 of PC Richard Turnham in the television police drama series *The Bill*, other television credits include *Coronation Street*, *Wycliffe*, *Goodnight Sweetheart* and *Silent Witness*.

Also on British television screens, **Nigel Humphreys** is the actor born in 1951 in Bognor Regis, Sussex.

With a range of credits that include *Dixon of Dock Green*, *Z-Cars*, *The Sweeney*, *Minder*, *Doctor Who* and *Birds of a Feather*, his big screen credits include the 1979 *Scum*, the 1980 *The Long Good Friday* and, from 1982, *Who Dares Wins*.

Best known for his comic personas of Dame Edna Everage and Sir Les Patterson, John Barry Humphries, better known as **Barry Humphries**, is the Australian comedian, actor, script writer, author and film producer born in 1934 in the Melbourne suburb of Kew.

The son of a construction worker, he graduated in laws and arts from Queen's College, Melbourne and became an exponent of the anarchic and 'absurdist' art movement known as Dada.

Having joined the Melbourne Theatre Company after graduation, he moved to London in 1959 and over the following decade collaborated with leading members of the British alternative comedy scene who included Spike Milligan, Peter Cook, Dudley Moore, Willie Rushton and Jonathan Miller.

A contributor to the satirical magazine *Private Eye*, then published by Peter Cook, one of his cartoon strip creations was *The Wonderful Life of Barry McKenzie* – with McKenzie an archetypal beer-swilling Australian 'bloke'.

His best known creations, however, are the Australian suburban 'housewife' Dame Edna Everage and the lecherous and drunken Australian 'cultural attaché' Sir Les Patterson – all played to great success by Humphries on stage, television and film.

On stage, he also appeared in 1967 as Fagin in the Piccadilly Theatre's revival of *Oliver!* while he also had a role, along with Cook and Moore, in the 1967 film *Bedazzled*.

The recipient of a host of honours and awards that include four BAFTA nominations, Officer of the Order of Australia for services to theatre and a CBE for services to entertainment, he announced his retirement from live entertainment in 2012.

A Welsh journalist, author and radio and

television presenter, Desmond John Humphrys, better known as **John Humphrys**, was born in the Cardiff working class district of Splott in 1943.

The son a self-employed French polisher and a hairdresser, he was aged fifteen when he left school to take up a job as a trainee reporter on the *Penarth Times*.

Later working for a time with the Cardiff-based *Western Mail* and then on a Welsh commercial television station, he joined the BBC in 1966 as the district reporter for Liverpool and the Northwest before working as a foreign correspondent in the United States and then South Africa.

Appointed BBC Diplomatic Correspondent in 1980, it was a year later that he became the main presenter of the flagship *Nine O'Clock News*, while other positions he has held include presenting the *Today* programme, the *On the Record* television programme and presenter of *Mastermind*.

An outspoken critic of what he has described as the 'dumbing-down' of British television and the misuse of the English language, he is the author of a number of books that include *Beyond Words* and *In God We Doubt: Confessions of a Failed Atheist*.

Also the recipient of a number of awards that include the 2003 Sony Gold Radio Award, he is the older brother of the late Welsh broadcaster **George Humphrys**.

Born in 1952 and becoming a journalist after studying at university, in common with his brother he also worked for a time with the *Western Mail*.

Joining BBC Radio Wales in 1978 and then moving to television and becoming a popular sports presenter, he was given a lifetime achievement award by BBC Wales at the Welsh Sports Personality of the Year Awards four years before his death in 2008 – and after having completed his autobiography *Not a Proper Journalist*.

Behind the camera lens, **Gerry Humphreys**, born in 1931 in Llandrindod, Powys, and who died in 2006, was the Welsh sound engineer who won Academy Award nominations for Best Sound for the 1982 film *Ghandi* and, from 1985, *A Chorus Line*.

In the creative world of the written word, **Emyr Humphreys** is the award-winning Welsh novelist, poet and playwright born in 1919 in Prestatyn, Flintshire.

Author of highly acclaimed works that include his 1958 novel *Hear and Forgive* – winner of the Somerset Maughan Award – the 1965 *Outside the House of Baal* and a sequence of novels, including *Bonds of Attachment*, that focus on the political and cultural history of his native land in the twentieth century, he is a Fellow of the Royal Society of Literature.

Also in Wales, Edward Morgan Humphreys,

better known as **E. Morgan Humphreys**, was the novelist, journalist and translator born in 1882 in Dyffryn Ardudwy, Gwynedd.

Writing under the pen-name "Celt", he contributed to the *Liverpool Daily Post* and the *Manchester Guardian*, while as a socialist he was a tutor for the Workers' Educational Association.

Recognised as one of the pioneers of the detective novel in Welsh and a member of the Royal Cambrian Academy of Art and the Welsh panel of the British Council, he died in 1955.

Winner of the 1984 Hemingway Foundation/ PEN Award for her *Dreams of Sleep*, **Josephine Humphreys** is the American novelist born in 1945 in Charleston, South Carolina.

A recipient of the American Academy of Arts and Letters Award in Literature, her 1987 novel *Rich in Love* was adapted for a film of the name, starring Albert Finney and Jill Clayburgh, in 1993.

Born in London in 1961 but now resident in Canada, **Helen Humphreys** is the novelist and poet whose novel *Leaving Earth* was selected as a *New York Times* Notable Book in 1998, while her 1990 *Anthem* won a Canadian Authors' Association Award for Poetry.

In the world of science, **Curtis Humphreys**,

born in 1898 in Alliance, Ohio, was the American physicist who, as chief of the radiometry section of the U.S. Navy during the 1940s, discovered what is named in his honour as the *Humphreys Series* relating to the spectroscopy of the hydrogen atom.

A recipient of the Naval Award for Achievement in Science, he died in 1986.

Bearers of the Humphreys name have also excelled in the highly competitive world of sport – not least in the rough and tumble that is the game of rugby.

Born in 1969 in Bridgend, Glamorgan, **Jonathan Humphreys** is the Welsh former international rugby union captain who, as a hooker, played club rugby for Kenfig Hill RFC, Cardiff and Bath.

Having been the forwards coach for Ospreys, he was appointed in the same role for the Scottish national side in 2013.

On Irish shores, **David Humphreys**, born in Belfast in 1971, is the retired rugby union player who, playing club rugby for Ulster, was the captain when it won the 1998-1999 Heineken Cup.

Capped 72 times for Ireland and the recipient of an MBE for his services to the sport, he is the older brother of the rugby union footballer **Ian Humphreys**, born in 1982.

Having played for Ulster and Leicester Tigers,

he captained the Irish team at the Rugby World Cup Sevens tournament in Hong Kong in 2005.

On the ice rink, Marika Humphreys, now better known by her married name of **Marika Humphreys-Baranova**, is the British former competitive ice dancer born in Chester in 1977.

Aged 15 when, partnered with Justin Lanning, she became the youngest skater ever to win the gold medal at the British Championships.

It was in 1998 that she teamed up with the Ukrainian ice dancer Vitaliy Baranova.

Marrying a year later, the couple went on to win events that include both the 2001 and 2002 British national titles and the 2002 Karl Schäfer Memorial.

On the fields of European football, **Ritchie Humphreys**, born in 1977 in Sheffield, is the English former footballer who, after playing for clubs that include Sheffield Wednesday, Cardiff City, Hartlepool, Port Vale and Chesterfield, was appointed chairman of the Professional Footballers Association in 2013.

Ranked 40th in 2009 in the *Daily Mail's* "Top 50 Teenage Sensations in Premier League History", his grandfather **Ernest Humphreys** played for clubs that include Millwall and Scottish clubs Motherwell and St Mirren.

From the football pitch to the golf course,

Warren Humphreys, born in 1952, is the English former professional player who won the 1971 English Amateur.

Winner of the 1985 Portuguese Open, he is now a television pundit on the game.

One particularly intrepid bearer of the proud name of Humphreys is the English professional sailor **Conrad Humphreys**, who has competed in three around the world races.

These are the 1993-1994 Whitbread Round the World Race, the 2000-2001 BT Global Challenge – in which he became the youngest winning skipper in the history of the race – and the 2004-2005 Vendée Globe.

The latter, a non-stop solo race around the world without assistance, is regarded as the toughest endurance race of any sport.